MY WORLD in ITALIAN

Coloring Book & Picture Dictionary

Tamara M. Mealer

PASSPORT BOOKS
NTC/Contemporary Publishing Group

To Parents and Teachers

Research has shown that the best way to help children learn a language is to involve them physically in the learning process. Entertaining, hands-on activities engage children's enthusiasm and encourage greater retention of learning.

My World in Italian has been created for today's young learner of Italian with these findings in mind. The coloring pages spark children's interest and involve them in hands-on activities. As children color, they will notice that some people or items in the pictures are numbered. They can look up the names of these people or items in Italian and English on the page opposite the picture. A pronunciation guide follows each Italian word to promote correct pronunciation. When the pictures have been colored, *My World in Italian* becomes a delightful picture dictionary that children have helped create themselves. Each picture is accompanied by a few questions designed to help children practice the words they are learning and encourage them to use the Italian names of items in the pictures. Use these questions as a guide for formulating more questions about the pictures and for starting conversations about the Italian words presented in each one. The more involved you become in a child's language-learning process, the more he or she will learn.

Published by Passport Books, a division of NTC Publishing Group.
© 1992 by NTC Publishing Group, 4255 West Touhy Avenue,
Lincolnwood (Chicago), Illinois 60646-1975 U.S.A.
9 ML 9 8 7 6

About This Book

This book will help you learn about your world in Italian. You will find pictures of places you know, like the classroom, the kitchen, the beach, the zoo, the circus, and many more. Color the pictures any way you like!

While you are coloring, you will notice numbers next to some objects or people in the picture. Look at the same numbers on the page across from the picture. You will find the names of the people and objects next to the numbers. First, you will see the names in Italian. After each Italian word, you will see a pronunciation guide in parentheses. This tells you how to say the Italian word aloud. It may look funny, but if you read it aloud, you will be saying the word correctly. To find out more about how to say sounds in Italian and using the pronunciation guides, read the section called "How to Say Italian Sounds." Last, you will also find the name of each person or object in English.

The pages across from the pictures also have some questions about what you see in the picture. Try to answer the questions with the Italian words you have learned. The answer key to the questions is in the back of the book, but don't peek until you have tried to answer the questions yourself!

At the beginning of the book, there are some facts about the Italian language. Knowing these will help you when you use the words you have learned to talk about things in Italian.

Share this book with your parents or with your friends. Learning Italian is a lot of fun, but you will enjoy it even more if you do it with a friend. *Divertiti!* (Have fun!)

Contents

Some Helpful Hints about Italian

Masculine and Feminine Words

In Italian, all nouns (names of people, places, and things) are either masculine or feminine. In this book, nouns have **la, il, lo,** or **l'** in front of them. These words all mean "the" in Italian.

Words that have **la** before them are feminine.

Example: la matita (pencil)

Words that have **il** before them are masculine.

Example: il cane (dog)

Some masculine words have **lo** before them. These words begin with **z** or with an **s** followed by a consonant.

Example: lo specchio (mirror)

If a word begins with a vowel in Italian, then you will see **l'** as in **l'albero** (tree). For these words, you simply learn by heart whether they are masculine or feminine.

Talking about More Than One

When you want to talk about more than one, you need to change the ending of the noun.

Most masculine nouns end in **-o.** To talk about more than one, change the **-o** to **-i.**

Example: il gatt**o** (cat)   i gatt**i** (cats)

Most feminine nouns end in **-a.** To talk about more than one, change the **-a** to **-e.**

Example: la tazz**a** (cup)   le tazz**e** (cups)

Some nouns end in **-e.** They may be either masculine or feminine. To talk about more than one, change the **-e** to **-i.**

Example: il can**e** (dog)   i can**i** (dogs)

The word **the** also changes when you talk about more than one. The word **il** changes to **i.**

Example: **il** cane (dog)   **i** cani (dogs)

The word **la** changes to **le.**

Example: **la** tazza (cup)   **le** tazze (cups)

The word **lo** changes to **gli.**

Example: **lo** sgabello (stool)   **gli** sgabelli (stools)

The word **l'** changes to **gli** for masculine words.

Example: **l'**albero (tree)   **gli** alberi (trees)

The word **l'** changes to **le** for feminine words.

Example: **l'**onda (wave)   **le** onde (waves)

How to Say Italian Sounds

Below is a list of Italian letters, with a guide to help you tell how to say each one. For each Italian letter, there is an English word that contains a sound close to that of the Italian letter.

In Italian, the letters usually stand for only one sound. This makes it easier for you to know how to say an Italian word when you see it in writing.

To practice saying sounds, read the English word aloud. Then practice saying the examples in Italian for each sound.

Vowels

a like the "a" in "father": **c̲a̲ne, g̲a̲tto**

e like the "e" in "chain": **tè̲, ma̲e̲stra, sol̲e̲**
or
like the "e" in "peck": **tre̲no, rastre̲llo**

i like the "i" in "machine": **l̲i̲bro, alber̲i̲**

o like the "o" in "sole": **sc̲o̲pa, pin̲o̲**
or
like the "o" in "north": **n̲o̲nna, c̲o̲lla**

u like the "oo" in "moon": **l̲u̲na, b̲u̲ca**

ai like the "igh" in "high": **fiora̲i̲o**

au like the "ow" in "how": **a̲u̲tista**

uo like the "oo" in "moon" + "o" in "sole": **f̲uo̲co, sc̲uo̲la**

Consonants

c before "a, o, u," like the "c" in "cat": **c̲ane, c̲olore, c̲ucchiai, for c̲a**
before "e, i," like the "ch" in "chin": **c̲estino, forbic̲i, bilanc̲ia**

ch like the "k" in "key": **panc̲h̲ina, zucc̲h̲ini, forc̲h̲etta**

g before "e, i," like the "j" in "jam": **g̲esso, g̲iacca, arg̲illa**
before other letters like the "g" in "go": **g̲atto, g̲omma, neg̲ozio, g̲ranturco**

gh like the "g" in "go": **ghiaccio**

gl like the "ll" in "million": **gli, coniglio, bottiglia**

gn like the "ni" in "onion": **lavagna, disegni**

s like the "s" in "sun": **sedia, busta, cestino**
or
like the "z" in "zoo": **vaso**

sc before "e, i," like the "sh" in "she": **scimmia, piscina, pesci**
before other letters, like the "sk" in "skin": **scopa, scarpe**

z like the "ts" in "pots": **zucchini, tazza**
or
like the "ds" in "beds": **mezzaluna**

Note: The letter "h" is not pronounced.

Using the Guide to Saying Words

In the book, each Italian word is followed by a guide to help you say the word.

In the guides, we've given special spellings to the sounds. Here is a list of the Italian letters. They are followed by the letters used in the guide to stand for them.

In each Italian word, there is one syllable (part of a word) that is said louder and more strongly than the other parts. In the guide, this syllable is in capital letters.

Italian Letters	Letters in the Guide
a	a
e (chain)	ay
e (peck)	eh
i	ee
o (sole)	oh
o (north)	o
u	oo
ai	igh
au	ow
uo	ooh

Note that **y** stands for the sound **ee** that is pronounced together, as one syllable, with the vowel that follows it.

c (before a, o, u)	k
c (before e, i)	ch
g (before a, o, u)	g
g (before e, i)	j
gl(i)	ly(ee)
gn	ny
s (sun)	s
ts (pots)	z
z (zoo)	z
z (ds)	ds

More Useful Words in Italian

Here are some useful words that are not included in the pictures.

I giorni della settimana

Days of the Week

lunedì	Monday
martedì	Tuesday
mercoledì	Wednesday
giovedì	Thursday
venerdì	Friday
sabato	Saturday
domenica	Sunday

I mesi

The Months

gennaio	January
febbraio	February
marzo	March
aprile	April
maggio	May
giugno	June
luglio	July
agosto	August
settembre	September
ottobre	October
novembre	November
dicembre	December

1. La nostra casa (la NOS-tra KA-sa) Our House

1. **le montagne** (lay mohn-TA-nyay) mountains
2. **gli alberi** (lyee AL-bay-ree) trees
3. **il muro di mattoni** (eel MOO-roh dee mat-TOH-nee) brick wall
4. **il pino** (eel PEE-noh) pine tree
5. **il garage** (eel ga-RAJ) garage
6. **la pietra** (la PYAY-tra) stone
7. **la piscina** (la pee-SHEE-na) swimming pool
8. **il forchettone** (il fohr-kayt-TOH-nay) gardening fork
9. **la paletta** (la pa-LAYT-ta) gardening shovel
10. **la buca** (la BOO-ka) hole
11. **la terra** (la TEHR-ra) soil
12. **la cassetta delle lettere** (la kas-SAYT-ta DAYL-lay LAYT-tay-ray) mailbox
13. **la carriola** (la kar-ree-O-la) wheelbarrow

14. **i fiori** (ee FYOH-ree)   flowers
15. **le foglie** (lay FO-lyay)   leaves
16. **il ramo** (eel RA-moh)   tree branch
17. **il canile** (eel ka-NEE-lay)   doghouse
18. **il cane** (eel KA-nay)   dog
19. **il giardiniere** (eel jar-dee-NYEH-ray)   gardener
20. **il rastrello** (eel ras-TREHL-loh)   rake
21. **la canna per innaffiare** (la KAN-na payr een-NAF-fya-ray)   watering hose
22. **l'ugello** (loo-JEHL-loh)   nozzle
23. **i mobili per la terrazza** (eel MOH-bee-lee payr la tayr-RAT-tsa)   patio furniture
24. **i cespugli** (ee chay-SPOO-lyee)   bushes
25. **le luci esterne** (lee LOO-chee ays-TEHR-nay)   outdoor lights
26. **il camino** (eel ca-MEE-noh)   chimney
27. **il tetto** (eel TAYT-toh)   roof
28. **la tegola** (la TAY-goh-la)   shingle
29. **la grondaia** (la grohn-DIGH-a)   gutter
30. **il vetro** (eel VAY-troh)   glass
31. **lo steccato** (loh stayk-KA-toh)   wooden fence

Questions

1. Name the two kinds of fences in the picture.   *il muro di mattoni*
2. What tools is the woman using?   *lo steccatto*
3. Why do you use "la canna per innaffiare"?
4. Who is raking the leaves?

la paletta, il forchettone
per i cespugli

il giardiniere

2. Il salotto (eel sa-LOT-toh)   The Living Room

1. **l'antenna** (lan-TAYN-na)   antenna
2. **la radio** (la RA-dyoh)   radio
3. **il giradischi** (eel jee-ra-DEES-key)   record player
4. **la macchina da scrivere** (la MAK-kee-na da SKREE-vay-ray)   typewriter
5. **i dischi** (ee DEES-key)   records
6. **il televisore** (eel tay-lay-vee-SOH-ray)   television set
7. **lo scaffale** (loh skaf-FA-lay)   bookcase
8. **il libro** (eel LEE-broh)   book
9. **il tappeto** (eel tap-PAY-toh)   carpet
10. **il telefono** (eel tay-LEH-foh-noh)   telephone
11. **il sofà** (eel soh-FA)   sofa
12. **i ferri da calza** (ee FEHR-ree da KAL-za)   knitting needles
13. **il filo** (eel FEE-loh)   yarn
14. **il tavolino** (eel ta-voh-LEE-noh)   coffee table
15. **la busta** (la BOOS-ta)   envelope
16. **la lettera** (la LAYT-tay-ra)   letter
17. **il giornale** (eel johr-NA-lay)   newspaper
18. **la nonna** (la NON-na)   grandmother
19. **il cuscino** (eel koo-SHEE-noh)   pillow
20. **l'aspirapolvere** (la-spee-ra-POHL-vay-ray)   vacuum cleaner
21. **la sedia a dondolo** (la SAY-dee-ah a DOHN-doh-loh)   rocking chair
22. **il nipote** (eel nee-POH-tay)   grandson
23. **il gatto** (eel GAT-toh)   cat

① —l'antenna
② —la radio
③ il giradischi
④
⑤ la makkena da skree vayray
i cischi
⑥ la il televisore
⑦ skafalea
⑧
la nona
⑨
⑩ il telefono
⑪
⑫
⑬
⑭
⑮ la busta
⑯
⑰ la letteca giornale (journal)
⑱
⑲ il cuscino (sh)
⑳ l'aspira polvere
㉑ la sedia a dondolo
㉒ il nipo
㉓
il gatto

24. **il cestino per i ceppi** (eel chays-TEE-noh payr ee CHAYP-pee)   log basket
25. **i ceppi** (ee CHAYP-pee)   logs
26. **la piastrella** (la pyas-TREHL-la)   floor tile
27. **il fuoco** (eel FOOH-koh)   fire
28. **la mensola** (la MEHN-soh-la)   mantel
29. **l'orologio** (lohr-oh-LO-joh)   clock
30. **il braccio portalampa** (eel BRA-chyoh pohr-ta-LAM-pa)   wall bracket
31. **il paralume** (eel pa-ra-LOO-may)   lampshade
32. **lo specchio** (loh SPEK-kee-oh)   mirror
33. **la cornice** (la kohr-NEE-chay)   frame
34. **le tende** (lay TAYN-day)   curtains
35. **l'ombrello** (loh-BREHL-loh)   umbrella
36. **il portaombrelli** (eel pohr-ta-ohm-BREHL-lee)   umbrella stand
37. **la poltrona** (la pohl-TROH-na)   armchair
38. **la pianta** (la PYAN-ta)   plant
39. **la foto** (la FO-toh)   photograph

Questions

1. What is on the coffee table?
2. What does the "nonna" have in her hands? – i ferri de calza
3. Who is playing with "il gatto"? – il nipote
4. What is on the mantel? – l'orologio
5. What is the boy near the shelves looking for?

il libro

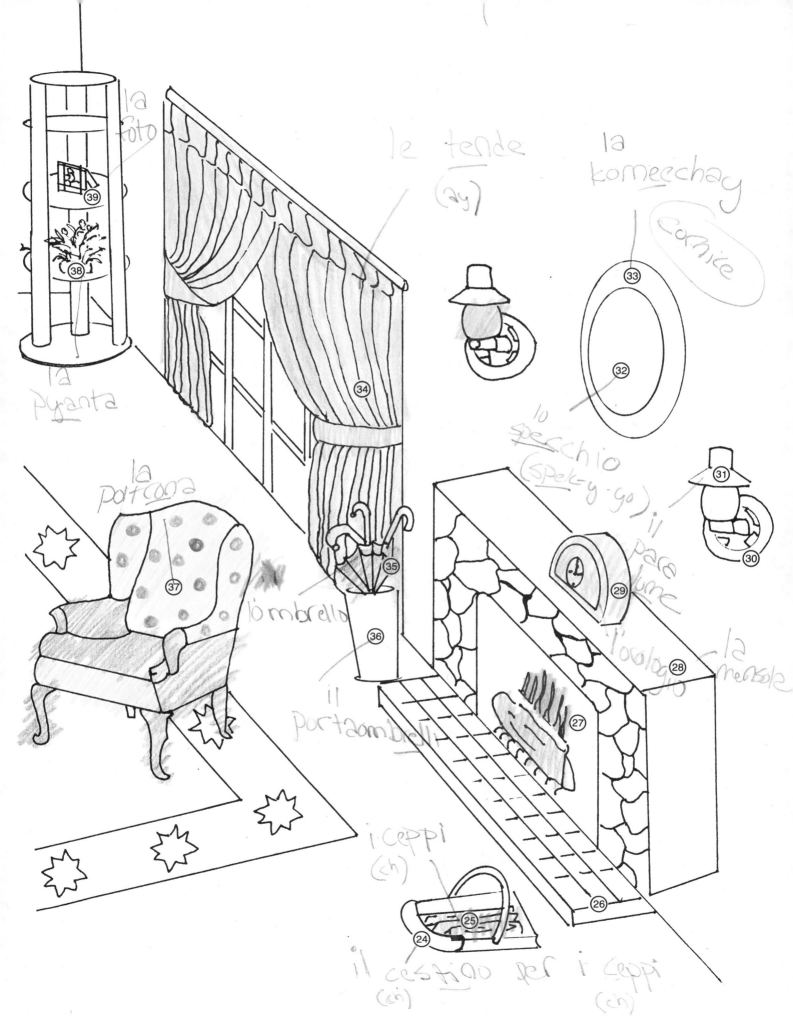

la foto

(39)

(38)

la pyanta

le tende (ay)

la korneechay

cornice

(33)

(32)

lo specchio (spek-y-go) il pare lume

(31)

(30)

la portcona

(37)

(34)

(29)

l'oologio

la mensola

(28)

(27)

lo mbrello

(35)

(36)

il portaombrelli

i ceppi (ch)

(24) (25)

(26)

il cestino per i ceppi (ch) (ch)

3. La cucina (la koo-CHEE-na)   The Kitchen

1. **il detersivo per i piatti** (eel day-tayr-SEE-voh payr ee PYAHT-tee)
   dish washing detergent
2. **la spazzola per i piatti** (la SPAT-tsoh-la payr ee PYAHT-tee)   dish brush
3. **l'armadietto da cucina** (lar-ma-DYAYT-toh da koo-CHEE-na)   kitchen cabinet
4. **il ricettario** (eel ree-chayt-TA-ryoh)   cookbook
5. **il lavandino** (eel la-van-DEE-noh)   sink
6. **il rubinetto** (eel roo-bee-NEHT-toh)   faucet
7. **la manopola del rubinetto** (la ma-NO-poh-la dayl roo-bee-NEHT-toh)   handle
8. **il tagliere** (eel ta-LYAY-ray)   cutting board
9. **il lavastoviglie** (eel la-va-stoh-VEE-lyay)   dishwasher
10. **il cassetto** (eel kas-SEHT-toh)   drawer
11. **la bomboletta spray** (la bohm-boh-LAYT-ta spray)   sprayer
12. **il polvere per lavare** (el POHL-vay-ray payr la-VA-ray)   cleanser
13. **i bicchieri** (ee beek-KYEH-ree)   glasses
14. **il matterello** (eel may-tay-REHL-loh)   rolling pin
15. **la scatoletta di carne** (la ska-toh-LAYT-ta dee KAR-nay)   canned meat
16. **il setaccio** (eel say-TA-chyo)   sifter
17. **il tostapane** (eel tohs-ta-PA-nay)   toaster
18. **il toast** (eel tohst)   toast
19. **la spatola** (la SPA-toh-la)   spatula
20. **la marmellata** (la mar-mayl-LA-ta)   jam
21. **il frullatore** (eel frool-la-TOH-ray)   blender
22. **il misurino** (eel mee-soo-REE-noh)   measuring cup
23. **la scodella** (la skoh-DEHL-la)   bowl
24. **il frullino a mano** (eel frool-LEE-no a MA-noh)   hand mixer
25. **la saliera** (la sa-LYEH-ra)   salt shaker
26. **la pepaiola** (la pay-pa-YO-la)   pepper shaker
27. **il mestolo** (eel MAYS-toh-loh)   ladle
28. **lo schiacciapatate** (loh skya-cha-pa-TA-tay)   potato masher
29. **i cucchiai per misurare** (ee kook-KYA-ee payr mee-soo-RA-ray)
    measuring spoons
30. **i tovaglioli di carta** (ee toh-va-LYO-lee dee KAR-ta)   paper napkins
31. **la forchetta** (la fohr-KAYT-ta)   fork
32. **il coltello** (eel cohl-TEHL-loh)   knife
33. **i cucchiai** (ee kook-KYA-ee)   spoons
34. **il burro** (eel BOOR-roh)   butter

35. **il cane** (eel KA-nay)   dog
36. **l'acqua** (LA-kwa)   water
37. **il caffè** (eel ka-FAY)   coffee
38. **il coperchio** (eel koh-PEHR-kyoh)   cover
39. **la scopa di filacce** (la SKOH-pa dee fee-LA-chay)   mop
40. **il secchio** (eel SAYK-kyoh)   bucket
41. **il cencio** (eel CHAYN-choh)   rag
42. **il roastbeef** (eel rohst beef)   roast beef
43. **il forno** (eel FOHR-noh)   oven
44. **la pentola** (la PAYN-toh-la)   pan
45. **il bollitore** (eel bohl-lee-TOH-ray)   tea kettle
46. **la cucina a fornello** (la koo-CHEE-na a fohr-NEHL-loh)   stove
47. **le uova** (lay OOH-va)   eggs
48. **la padella** (la pa-DEHL-la)   frying pan
49. **la madre** (la MAD-ray)   mother
50. **la paletta per la spazzatura** (la pa-LAYT-ta payr la spat-tsa-TOO-ra)   dustpan
51. **la pattumiera** (la pat-too-MYEH-ra)   trash can
52. **il frigorifero** (eel free-goh-REE-fay-roh)   refrigerator
53. **la torcia elettrica** (la TOR-cha ay-LEHT-tree-ka)   flashlight
54. **il congelatore** (eel kohn-jay-la-TOH-ray)   freezer
55. **lo strofinaccio** (loh stroh-fee-NA-chyo)   dish cloth
56. **il detersivo** (eel day-tayr-SEE-voh)   laundry detergent
57. **la lavatrice** (la la-va-TREE-chay)   washing machine
58. **l'essiccatore** (lays-seek-ka-TOH-ray)   dryer
59. **la scopa** (la SKOH-pa)   broom
60. **il portalettere** (eel pohr-ta-LAYT-tay-ray)   letter holder
61. **il cestino da picnic** (eel chays-TEE-noh da PEEK-neek)   picnic basket
62. **il secchiello da ghiaccio** (eel SAYK-kee-ehl-loh da GYA-choh)   ice bucket
63. **le tazze** (lay TAT-tsay)   cups

Questions

1. What is in "il forno"?
2. What is "il cane" drinking?
3. What is in the toaster?
4. What is in the bucket?
5. What might you use to make a cake?

4. Nell'aula (nayl-AW-la)   In the Classroom

1. **il dinosauro** (eel dee-noh-SAW-roh)   dinosaur
2. **l'orologio** (lor-oh-LO-joh)   clock
3. **il soffitto** (eel sohf-FEE-toh)   ceiling
4. **l'alfabeto** (la-fa-BEH-toh)   alphabet
5. **la cattedra** (la KAT-tay-dra)   teacher's desk
6. **il vaso** (eel VA-zoh)   vase
7. **il coniglio** (eel kohn-NEE-lyoh)   rabbit
8. **la lavagna** (la la-VA-nya)   blackboard
9. **la sottrazione** (la soht-tra-ZYOH-nay)   subtraction
10. **la moltiplicazione** (la mohl-tee-plee-ka-ZYOH-nay)   multiplication
11. **l'addizione** (lad-dee-ZYOH-nay)   addition
12. **lo spogliatoio** (loh spoh-lya-TOH-yoh)   closet
13. **il calendario** (eel ka-layn-DA-ryoh)   calendar
14. **la foto** (la FO-toh)   photograph
15. **le biglie** (lay BEE-lyay)   marbles
16. **il mappamondo** (eel map-pa-MOHN-doh)   globe
17. **i libri** (ee LEE-bree)   books
18. **le bambole** (lay BAM-boh-lay)   dolls
19. **le scatole** (lay SKA-toh-lay)   boxes
20. **la colla** (la COL-la)   glue
21. **il pupazzo di carta** (eel poo-PAT-tsoh dee KAR-ta)   paper puppet
22. **il sacchetto di carta** (eel sak-KAYT-toh dee KAR-ta)   paper bag
23. **il nastro adesivo** (eel NAS-troh a-day-SEE-voh)   adhesive tape
24. **le forbici** (lay FOR-bee-chee)   scissors
25. **l'argilla** (lar-JEEL-la)   clay
26. **la gabbia** (la GAB-bya)   cage

ABCDEFGHIJKLMNOPQRSTU

$$+\,375$$
$$149$$

$$409$$
$$\times 8$$

$$-\,583$$
$$250$$

27. **i pastelli** (ee pas-TEHL-lee)   crayons
28. **il regolo** (eel REH-goh-loh)   ruler
29. **il pennello** (eel payn-NEHL-loh)   paintbrush
30. **il gesso** (eel JAYS-soh)   chalk
31. **il colore** (eel koh-LOHR-ray)   paint
32. **le puntine da disegno** (lay poo-TEE-nay da dee-SAY-nyoh)   tacks
33. **i cubetti** (ee coo-BAYT-tee)   building blocks
34. **il cavalletto** (eel ca-val-LAYT-toh)   easel
35. **l'acquerello** (lak-kwa-REHL-loh)   watercolor
36. **il grembiule** (eel graym-BYOO-lay)   smock
37. **la gomma** (la GOHM-ma)   eraser
38. **la carta** (la KAR-ta)   paper
39. **le matite** (lay ma-TEE-tay)   pencils
40. **l'alunno** (la-LOON-noh)   student
41. **il cestino** (eel chays-TEE-noh)   wastebasket
42. **i disegni** (ee dee-SAY-nyee)   drawings
43. **l'acquario** (lak-KWA-ryoh)   aquarium
44. **i pesci** (ee PAY-shee)   fish
45. **la finestra** (la fee-NAYS-tra)   window
46. **il maiale** (eel ma-YA-lay)   pig
47. **l'uccello** (loo-CHAYL-loh)   bird
48. **il gatto** (eel GAT-toh)   cat
49. **la scimmia** (la SHEEM-mya)   monkey
50. **la cartina geografica** (la kar-TEE-na jay-oh-GRA-fee-ka)   map
51. **il temperamatite** (eel taym-pay-ra-ma-TEE-tay)   pencil sharpener
52. **il portamatite** (eel pohr-ta-ma-TEE-tay)   pencil holder
53. **il quaderno** (eel kwa-DEHR-noh)   notebook
54. **la maestra** (la MA-ays-tra)   teacher

Questions

1. What do you use to cut paper?
2. Name the three kinds of math problems on the board.
3. What is the girl at the easel wearing?
4. Name the objects hanging on the left wall.

5. I vestiti (ee vays-TEE-tee)   Clothing

1. **il cappello** (eel kap-PEHL-loh)   hat
2. **gli occhiali** (lyee ok-KYA-lee)   glasses
3. **il vestito** (eel vays-TEE-toh)   dress
4. **il costume da bagno** (eel kohs-TOO-may da BA-nyoh)   bathing suit
5. **la borsa** (la BOHR-sa)   purse
6. **gli stivali da neve** (lyee stee-VA-lee da NAY-vay)   snow boots
7. **le pantofole** (lay pan-TO-foh-lay)   slippers
8. **le scarpe col tacco alto** (lay SKAR-pay kol TAK-koh AL-toh)   high-heeled shoes
9. **il maglione** (eel ma-LYOH-nay)   sweater
10. **la gonna** (la GOHN-na)   skirt
11. **le scarpe** (lay SKAR-pay)   shoes
12. **i sandali** (ee SAN-da-lee)   sandals

13. **la giacca a vento** (la JAK-ka a VEHN-to)   jacket
14. **il cappello** (eel kap-PEHL-loh)   cap
15. **la giacca** (la JAK-ka)   suit coat
16. **la cravatta** (la kra-VAT-ta)   tie
17. **il farfallino** (eel far-fal-LEE-noh)   bow tie
18. **l'impermeabile** (leem-payr-may-A-bee-lay)   rain coat
19. **la camicia a maniche lunghe** (la ka-MEE-cha a MA-nee-kay LOON-gay)
    long-sleeved shirt
20. **il gilè** (eel gee-LAY)   vest
21. **la cintura** (la sheen-TOO-ra)   belt
22. **l'accappatoio** (lak-kap-pa-TOH-yoh)   bathrobe
23. **i pantaloni** (ee pan-ta-LOH-nee)   pants
24. **le mutande** (lay moo-TAN-day)   underpants
25. **le calze** (lay KAL-zay)   socks
26. **il pigiama** (eel pee-JA-ma)   pajamas
27. **le scarpe da tennis** (lay SKAR-pay da TEHN-nees)   tennis shoes

Questions

1. What do you wear to see better?
2. What do you wear to bed?
3. What do you wear inside your shoes?
4. What do you wear to go swimming?

6. Le stagioni e il tempo (lay sta-JOH-nee ay eel TEHM-poh)
The Seasons and the Weather

1. **l'estate** (lays-TA-tay)   summer
2. **la primavera** (la pree-ma-VEH-ra)   spring
3. **l'inverno** (leen-VEHR-noh)   winter
4. **l'autunno** (low-TOON-noh)   autumn

5. **il sole** (eel SOH-lay)   sun
6. **le nuvole** (lay NOO-voh-lay)   clouds
7. **la luna** (la LOO-na)   moon
8. **l'arcobaleno** (lar-koh-ba-LAY-no)   rainbow
9. **caldo** (KAL-doh)   hot
10. **il fulmine** (eel FOOL-mee-nay)   lightning
11. **la pioggia** (la PYO-ja)   rain
12. **freddo** (FRAYD-doh)   cold
13. **la neve** (la NAY-vay)   snow

Questions

1. What do you see after it rains?
2. What is the warmest season of the year?
3. What do you see during a thunderstorm?
4. What do you see in the sky at night?

7. Gli sport (lyee sport)   Sports

1. **la scherma** (la SKAYR-ma)   fencing
2. **il tennis** (eel TEHN-nees)   tennis
3. **la lotta sportiva** (la LOT-ta spor-TEE-va)   wrestling
4. **il ciclismo** (eel chee-KLEEZ-moh)   cycling
5. **lo sci** (loh shee)   skiing
6. **il bowling** (eel BOOHL-ing)   bowling
7. **la pallacanestro** (la pal-la-ka-NEHS-troh)   basketball

8. **il pugilato** (eel poo-jee-LA-toh) boxing
9. **il baseball** (eel bayees-ball) baseball
10. **il judo** (eel JOO-doh) judo
11. **lo sci nautico** (loh shee NOW-tee-koh) waterskiing
12. **il football americano** (eel FOOT-ball a-may-ree-KA-no) football

Questions

1. For which sport do you need a bat?
2. For which sports do you need skis?
3. Name a sport for which you need a bicycle.
4. Which sports use a ball?

8. La città (la cheet-TA)   The City

1. l'edificio (lay-dee-FEE-chyoh)   building
2. il fioraio (eel fyoh-RIGH-oh)   florist's
3. il negozio di giocattoli (eel nay-GO-zyoh dee joh-KAT-toh-lee)   toy store
4. la fermata dell'autobus (la fayr-MA-ta dayl OW-toh-boos)   bus stop
5. la panchina (la pan-KEY-na)   bench
6. il panetteria (eel pa-nayt-tay-REE-a)   bakery
7. la tenda esterna (la TAYN-da ays-TEHR-na)   awning
8. il pedone (eel pay-DOH-nay)   pedestrian
9. lo scuolabus (loh SKOOH-la-boos)   school bus
10. l'autista (low-TEES-ta)   bus driver
11. il furgone (eel foor-GOH-nay)   van
12. il semaforo (eel say-MA-foh-roh)   traffic light
13. il tassì (eel tas-SEE)   taxi
14. la strada (la STRA-da)   street
15. il camion (eel KA-myohn)   truck
16. la stazione di servizio (la sta-ZYOH-nay dee sayr-VEE-zyoh)   gas station
17. la pompa di benzina (la POHM-pa dee bayn-ZEE-na)   gas pump

18. **il passaggio pedonale** (eel pas-SA-joh pay-doh-NA-lay) pedestrian crossing
19. **il bulldozer** (eel BOOL-doh-zehr) bulldozer
20. **il tubo** (eel TOO-boh) pipe
21. **la buca** (la BOOH-ka) hole
22. **la cassetta delle lettere** (la kas-SAYT-ta DAYL-lay LAYT-tay-ray) mailbox
23. **il lampione** (eel lam-PYOH-nay) streetlight
24. **il vigile del fuoco** (eel VEE-gee-lay dayl FOOH-koh) fire fighter
25. **l'ascia** (LA-cha) ax
26. **la scala** (la SKA-la) ladder
27. **l'autopompa** (low-toh-POHM-pa) fire truck
28. **il poliziotto** (eel poh-lee-ZYOT-toh) police officer
29. **la collisione** (la kohl-lee-ZYON-nay) collision
30. **la sirena** (la see-REH-na) siren
31. **la macchina della polizia** (la MAK-kee-na DAYL-la poh-lee-ZEE-a) police car
32. **l'idrante** (lee-DRAN-tay) fire hydrant
33. **l'albero** (LAL-bay-roh) tree
34. **l'ambulanza** (lam-boo-LAN-za) ambulance
35. **il carro attrezzi** (eel KAR-roh at-TRAYT-tsee) tow truck
36. **il parchimetro** (eel par-KEE-may-troh) parking meter
37. **il parco giochi** (eel PAR-koh JOH-kee) playground

Questions

1. What happened to the two cars in the intersection?
2. If you are hurt in an accident, what takes you to the hospital?
3. Who is directing traffic?
4. What is "il vigile del fuoco"?

9. Al supermercato (al soo-payr-mayr-KA-toh)   At the Supermarket

1. **il gelato** (eel jay-LA-toh)   ice cream
2. **la bottiglia** (la boht-TEE-lyah)   bottle
3. **lo zucchero** (loh ZOOK-kay-roh)   sugar
4. **il burro d'arachidi** (eel BOOR-roh da-RA-kee-dee)   peanut butter
5. **il gelato al cioccolato** (eel jay-LA-toh al chyoh-koh-LA-toh)   chocolate ice cream
6. **la scatola** (la SKA-toh-la)   can
7. **il carrello** (eel kar-REHL-loh)   shopping cart
8. **la marmellata** (la mar-mayl-LA-ta)   jam
9. **il pane** (eel PA-nay)   bread
10. **la bilancia** (la bee-LAN-cha)   scale
11. **le ciliege** (lay chee-LYAY-jay)   cherries
12. **i lamponi** (ee lam-POH-nee)   raspberries
13. **l'uva** (LOO-va)   grapes
14. **le banane** (lay ba-NA-nay)   bananas
15. **le papaie** (lay pa-PA-yay)   papayas
16. **le fragole** (lay FRA-goh-lay)   strawberries
17. **la frutta** (la FROOT-ta)   fruit
18. **il negoziante** (eel nay-goh-zee-AN-tay)   grocer
19. **la spesa** (la SPAY-sa)   groceries
20. **il sacco di carta** (eel SAK-koh dee KAR-ta)   paper bag
21. **la cassiera** (la kas-SYAY-ra)   cashier
22. **la cassa** (la KAS-sa)   cash register
23. **lo scontrino** (loh scohn-TREE-noh)   receipt
24. **il cestino per la spesa** (eel chays-TEE-noh payr la SPAY-sa)   grocery basket

PANE

FRUTTA

25. **le patate** (lay pa-TA-tay) potatoes
26. **le carote** (lay ka-RO-tay) carrots
27. **le cipolle** (lay shee-POHL-lay) onions
28. **i fagiolini** (ee fa-joh-LEE-nee) beans
29. **i pomodori** (ee poh-moh-DO-ree) tomatoes
30. **i cavoli** (ee KA-voh-lee) cabbages
31. **le melanzane** (lay may-lan-ZA-nay) eggplants
32. **la lattuga** (la lat-TOO-ga) lettuce
33. **il granturco** (eel gran-TOOR-koh) corn
34. **le pere** (lay PEH-ray) pears
35. **gli zucchini** (lyee zook-KEE-nee) squash
36. **gli asparagi** (lyee as-PA-ra-gee) asparagus
37. **i peperoni** (ee pay-pay-ROH-nee) bell peppers
38. **i cavolfiori** (ee ka-vohl-FYOH-ree) cauliflower
39. **le prugne** (lay PROO-nyay) plums
40. **i limoni** (ee lee-MOH-nee) lemons
41. **le pesche** (lay PEHS-kay) peaches
42. **le mele** (lay MAY-lay) apples
43. **la torta** (la TOHR-ta) cake
44. **la torta** (la TOHR-ta) pie
45. **le paste** (lay PAS-tay) pastry
46. **il tonno** (eel TOHN-noh) tuna
47. **il succo** (eel SOOK-koh) juice
48. **la crema per le mani** (la CRAY-ma payr lay MA-nee) hand cream
49. **la farina** (la fa-REE-na) flour
50. **i cereali** (ee chay-ree-A-lee) cereal
51. **lo scaffale** (loh skaf-FA-lay) shelf
52. **il lavoratore** (eel la-voh-ra-TOH-ray) worker
53. **i biscotti** (ee bees-KOT-tee) cookies
54. **il latte** (eel LAT-tay) milk
55. **il formaggio** (eel fohr-MA-joh) cheese
56. **le salsiccie** (lay sal-SEE-chay) sausages
57. **le uova** (lay OOH-va) eggs
58. **l'agnello** (la-NYEHL-loh) lamb
59. **il burro** (eel BOOR-roh) butter
60. **il pollo** (eel POHL-loh) chicken
61. **i granchi** (ee GRAN-kee) crabs
62. **il pesce** (eel PAY-chay) fish

Questions

1. What is the girl getting from the freezer?
2. Name all the fruits and vegetables that start with the letter "c."
3. Who is behind the cash register?
4. In what do you put your groceries as you walk through the store?
5. In what do you put your groceries to take them home?

10. Al ristorante (al rees-tohr-AN-tay)   In the Restaurant

1. **la pianta** (la PYAN-ta)   plant
2. **il vaso** (eel VA-zoh)   pot
3. **il camino** (eel ka-MEE-noh)   fireplace
4. **la tavola** (la TA-voh-la)   table
5. **la sedia** (la SEH-dya)   chair
6. **il bicchiere** (eel beek-KYEH-ray)   glass
7. **il piatto** (eel PYAT-toh)   plate
8. **la tovaglia** (la toh-VA-lya)   tablecloth
9. **la cameriera** (la kam-ay-RYAY-ra)   waitress
10. **l'insalata** (leen-sa-LA-ta)   salad
11. **le mollette** (lay mohl-layt-tay)   tongs
12. **il ghiaccio** (eel GYA-choh)   ice
13. **la bistecca** (la bees-TAYK-ka)   steak
14. **la torta** (la TOHR-ta)   cake
15. **la pancetta** (la pan-CHAYT-ta)   bacon
16. **le uova fritte** (lay OOH-va FREET-tay)   fried eggs
17. **la teiera** (la tay-YEH-ra)   teapot
18. **il pollo arrosto** (eel POHL-loh ar-ROS-toh)   roast chicken
19. **la brocca** (la BROK-ka)   pitcher
20. **il conto** (eel KOHN-toh)   bill
21. **la marmellata** (la mar-mayl-LA-ta)   jam
22. **il menu** (eel MEH-noo)   menu
23. **il sale** (eel SA-lay)   salt
24. **il pepe** (eel PAY-pay)   pepper
25. **il piattino** (eel pyat-TEE-noh)   saucer
26. **la tazza** (la TAT-tsa)   cup
27. **il tovagliolo** (eel toh-va-LYOH-loh)   napkin
28. **il panino** (eel pa-NEE-noh)   sandwich
29. **l'hamburger** (LAM-boo-gayr)   hamburger

30. **le salsiccie** (lay sal-SEE-chay)   sausages
31. **il salame** (eel sa-LA-may)   salami
32. **il cuoco** (eel KOOH-koh)   chef
33. **il grembiule** (eel graym-BYOO-lay)   apron
34. **la scodella di metallo** (eel skoh-DEHL-la dee may-TAL-loh)   metal bowl
35. **il prosciutto** (eel proh-SHOOT-toh)   ham
36. **le uova ripiene** (lay OOH-va ree-PYAY-nay)   stuffed eggs
37. **il calice** (eel KA-lee-chay)   goblet
38. **il tè** (eel tay)   tea
39. **l'affettatrice** (laf-fayt-ta-TREE-chay)   meat slicer
40. **il lavandino** (eel la-van-DEE-noh)   sink
41. **i piatti sporchi** (ee PYAT-tee SPOHR-kee)   dirty dishes
42. **la caffettiera** (la kaf-fayt-TYEH-ra)   coffeepot

Questions

1. Who is cooking in the kitchen?
2. Who is carrying the salad bowl?
3. What is the boy eating?
4. What does the girl have in her hands?
5. What do you use to wipe your hands?

11. La posta (la POS-ta)   The Post Office

1. **la bandiera** (la ban-DYAY-ra)   flag
2. **la posta** (la POS-ta)   post office
3. **la rampa di scarica** (la RAM-pa dee SKA-ree-ka)   loading dock
4. **l'entrata** (layn-TRA-ta)   entrance
5. **il camion dalla posta** (eel KA-myohn DAYL-la POS-ta)   mail truck
6. **la cassetta delle lettere** (la kas-SAYT-ta DAYL-lay LAYT-tay-ray)   mailbox
7. **il postino** (eel pohs-TEE-noh)   mail carrier
8. **il sacco della posta** (eel SAK-koh DAYL-la POS-ta)   mail bag
9. **il prezzo** (eel PRAYT-tsoh)   price
10. **la bilancia** (la bee-LAN-cha)   scale
11. **il pacchetto** (eel pak-KAYT-toh)   package
12. **il francobollo** (eel fran-koh-BOHL-loh)   stamp
13. **la lettera** (la LAY-tay-ra)   letter
14. **l'indirizzo** (leen-dee-REET-tsoh)   address
15. **l'impiegata postale** (leem-pyay-GA-tah pohs-TA-lay)   postal worker
16. **il pacco di lettere** (eel PAK-koh dee LAYT-tay-ray)   bundled letters
17. **il giornale** (eel johr-NA-lay)   newspaper
18. **la rivista** (la ree-VEES-ta)   magazine

Questions

1. Where do you go to mail letters?
2. What must you put on a letter before you mail it?
3. Who delivers the mail?
4. What is "la rivista"?

12. La banca (la BAN-ka)   The Bank

1. **lo schedario** (loh skay-DA-ryoh)   file cabinet
2. **il quadro** (eel KWA-droh)   painting
3. **il custode** (eel koos-TOH-day)   guard
4. **la cassaforte** (la kas-sa-FOHR-tay)   safe
5. **la cassetta di sicurezza** (la kas-SAYT-ta dee see-koo-RAYT-tsa)
   safety deposit box
6. **il cliente** (eel KLEE-ehn-tay)   client
7. **il libretto degli assegni** (eel lee-BRAYT-toh DAY-lyee as-SAY-nyee)   checkbook
8. **la carta di credito** (la KAR-ta dee CRAY-dee-toh)   credit card
9. **i biglietti** (eel bee-LYAY-tee)   bills
10. **le monete** (lay moh-NAY-tay)   coins
11. **il modulo per i depositi** (eel MO-doo-loh payr ee day-PO-see-tee)   deposit slip
12. **la penna** (la PAYN-na)   pen
13. **l'assegno** (las-SAY-nyoh)   check
14. **il sacchetto per i soldi** (eel sak-KAYT-toh payr ee SOL-dee)   money bag
15. **il cassiere** (eel kas-SYEH-ray)   bank teller

Questions

1. What can people use to pay a bill without using cash?
2. Name the place where money is kept in a bank.
3. Who is standing near the vault?
4. What do you use to make a deposit?

13. Dal medico (dal MAY-dee-koh) At the Doctor's

1. **la pressione arteriosa** (la prays-ZYOH-nay ar-tay-ree-OH-sa) blood pressure
2. **l'infermiere** (leen-fayr-MYAY-ray) nurse
3. **l'orologio da polso** (lohr-oh-LO-joh da POHL-soh) wristwatch
4. **il termometro** (eel tayr-MO-may-troh) thermometer
5. **l'ago** (LA-goh) needle
6. **la siringa** (la see-REEN-ga) syringe
7. **le pillole** (lay PEEL-loh-lay) pills
8. **il tecnico** (eel TAYK-nee-koh) technician
9. **il guanto** (eel GWAN-toh) glove
10. **il gesso** (eel JAYS-soh) cast
11. **la tabella per l'esame della vista**
    (la ta-BEHL-la payr lay-SA-may DEL-la VEES-ta) eye chart
12. **l'esame d'udito** (lay-SA-may doo-DEE-toh) hearing test
13. **l'otoscopio** (loh-tohs-KO-pyoh) otoscope
14. **il bambino** (eel bam-BEE-noh) baby
15. **lo stetoscopio** (loh stay-tohs-KOH-pyoh) stethoscope
16. **il pediatra** (eel pay-DYA-tra) pediatrician
17. **la ricetta** (la ree-CHAYT-ta) prescription

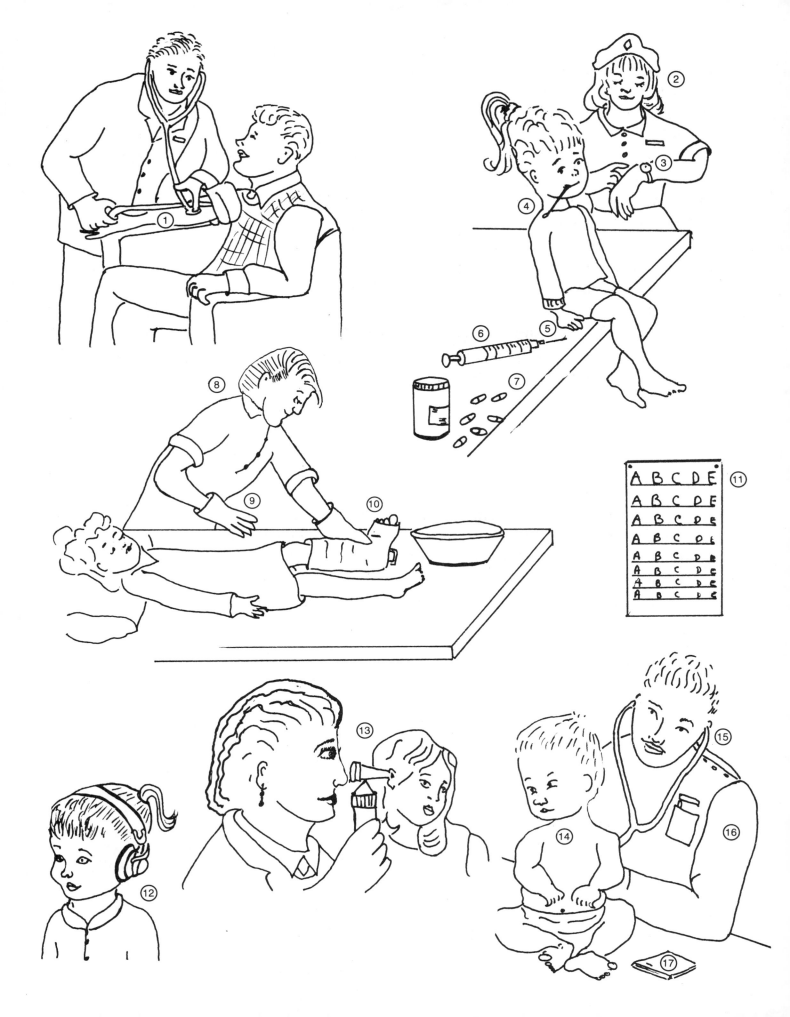

18. **l'otturazione** (loht-too-ra-ZYOH-nay)   filling
19. **il trapano** (eel TRA-pa-noh)   drill
20. **la carie** (la KA-ryay)   cavity
21. **gli strumenti dentali** (lyee stroo-MAYN-tee dayn-TA-lee)   dental instruments
22. **l'apparecchio per i denti** (lap-pa-RAYK-kyoh payr ee DEHN-tee)   braces
23. **la radiografia** (la ra-dyoh-gra-FEE-a)   X ray
24. **l'ortopedico** (lohr-toh-PEH-dee-koh)   orthopedist
25. **la benda** (la BAYN-da)   bandage
26. **il veterinario** (eel vay-tay-ree-NA-ryoh)   veterinarian
27. **l'ascensore** (la-chayn-SOH-ray)   elevator
28. **la sala d'aspetto** (la SA-la das-PEHT-toh)   waiting room
29. **le gruccie** (lay GROO-chay)   crutches
30. **il calendario** (eel ka-layn-DA-ryoh)   calendar
31. **la segretaria** (la say-gray-TA-ree-a)   receptionist
32. **l'appuntamento** (lap-poon-ta-MAYN-toh)   appointment

Questions

1. Who is taking the girl's temperature?
2. What instrument is the doctor using to listen to the baby's heart?
3. What is the name for an animal doctor?
4. What are "le gruccie"?
5. What does the doctor write for you when you need medicine?

14. La stazione di servizio

(la sta-ZYOH-nay dee sayr-VEE-zyoh)   The Service Station

1. **la gru idraulica** (la groo ee-DROW-lee-ka)   hydraulic lift
2. **il parabrezza incrinato** (eel pa-ra-BRAYD-dza een-kree-NA-toh)
   cracked windshield
3. **l'autolavaggio** (law-toh-la-VA-joh)   car wash
4. **lo sportello ammaccato** (loh spohr-TEHL-loh am-mak-KA-toh)   dented door
5. **il carro attrezzi** (eel KAR-roh at-TRAYT-tsee)   tow truck
6. **la pompa di benzina** (la POHM-pa dee bayn-ZEE-na)   gas pump
7. **il benzinaio** (eel bayn-zee-NIGH-oh)   attendant
8. **il bidone per la benzina** (eel bee-DOH-nay payr la bayn-ZEE-na)   gas can
9. **il coperchio del serbatoio** (eel koh-PEHR-kyoh dayl sayr-ba-TOY-oh)   gas cap
10. **il bagagliaio** (eel ba-ga-LYIGH-oh)   trunk
11. **il tetto** (ee TAYT-toh)   roof
12. **il sedile** (ee say-DEE-lay)   seat
13. **lo sportello** (loh spohr-TEHL-loh)   door
14. **la gomma** (la GOHM-ma)   tire
15. **la targa** (la TAR-ga)   license plate
16. **il paraurti** (eel pa-ra-OOR-tee)   bumper
17. **il fanale** (eel fa-NA-lay)   headlight
18. **il cofano** (eel CO-fa-noh)   hood
19. **il tergicristallo** (eel tayr-jee-krees-TAL-loh)   windshield wiper
20. **il volante** (eel voh-LAN-tay)   steering wheel

21. **il oliatore** (eel oh-lya-TOH-ray)   oil can
22. **il radiatore** (eel ra-dya-TOH-ray)   radiator
23. **la cassetta degli attrezzi** (la kays-SAYT-ta DAY-lyee at-TRAYT-tsee)   toolbox
24. **la batteria** (la bat-tay-REE-a)   battery
25. **i cavi per l'avviamento** (ee KA-vee payr av-vee-a-MAYN-toh)   jumper cables
26. **il cacciavite** (eel ka-cha-VEE-tay)   screwdriver
27. **il martello** (eel mar-TEHL-loh)   hammer
28. **la chiave** (la KYA-vay)   wrench
29. **il dado** (eel DA-doh)   nut
30. **la vite** (la VEE-tay)   screw
31. **la ruota** (la ROOH-ta)   wheel
32. **l'estintore** (lays-teen-TOH-ray)   fire extinguisher
33. **le gomme** (lay GOHM-may)   tires
34. **la pompa pneumatica** (la POHM-pa pnayoo-MA-tee-ka)   air pump
35. **la gomma a terra** (la GOHM-ma a TEHR-ra)   flat tire
36. **il meccanico** (eel mayk-KA-nee-koh)   mechanic

Questions

1. What is the name for a person who repairs cars?
2. What is "il paraurti"?
3. What is the name for the truck you see in the picture?
4. Name a place where people take cars to have them washed.
5. Where in a car can you put suitcases?

15. Il trasporto (eel tras-POR-toh) Transportation

1. **la monorotaia** (la moh-noh-roh-TA-ya) monorail
2. **il treno** (eel TREH-noh) train
3. **la funicolare** (la foo-nee-koh-LA-ray) cable car
4. **la macchina** (la MAK-kee-na) automobile
5. **il camion** (eel KA-myohn) truck
6. **l'autobus** (LOW-toh-boos) bus
7. **la motocicletta** (la moh-toh-chee-KLAYT-ta) motorcycle
8. **la bicicletta** (la bee-chee-KLAYT-ta) bicycle

9. **l'aereo** (la-EH-ray-oh) airplane
10. **il pallone aereostatico** (eel pal-LOH-nay a-eh-ray-oh-STA-tee-ko) hot-air balloon
11. **il paracadute** (eel pa-ra-ka-DOO-tay) parachute
12. **il missile** (eel MIS-see-lay) rocket
13. **l'elicottero** (lay-lee-KOT-tay-roh) helicopter
14. **la nave** (la NA-vay) ship
15. **la barca** (la BAR-ka) boat
16. **il sottomarino** (eel soht-toh-ma-REE-noh) submarine
17. **la chiatta** (la KYA-ta) barge
18. **la canoa** (la ka-NO-a) canoe

Questions

1. What should you have with you if you jump out of an airplane?
2. Name two vehicles with two wheels.
3. Name a vehicle that travels under water.
4. What vehicle in the picture can go to the moon?

16. La fattoria (la fat-toh-REE-a)   The Farm

1. il prato (eel PRA-toh)   field
2. il mulino a vento (eel moo-LEE-no a VEHN-toh)   windmill
3. la collina (la kohl-LEE-na)   hill
4. la valle (la VAL-lay)   valley
5. la cascata (la kas-KA-ta)   waterfall
6. il granaio (eel gra-NIGH-oh)   barn
7. la chiesa (la KYAY-sa)   church
8. il campanile (eel kam-pa-NEE-lay)   bell tower
9. il villino (eel veel-LEE-noh)   cottage
10. la ruota del mulino (la ROOH-ta dayl moo-LEE-noh)   waterwheel
11. il fieno (eel FYEH-noh)   hay
12. il recinto (eel ray-CHEEN-toh)   corral
13. la stalla (la STAL-la)   stable
14. il barile (eel ba-REE-lay)   barrel
15. il toro (eel TOH-roh)   bull
16. il laccio (eel LA-choh)   lasso
17. il cowboy (eel KOW-boy)   cowboy
18. il cavallo (eel ka-VAL-loh)   horse
19. il cappello da cowboy (eel kap-PEHL-loh da KOW-boy)   cowboy hat
20. la sella (la SEHL-la)   saddle
21. la mucca (la MOOK-ka)   cow
22. la contadina (la kon-ta-DEE-na)   farmer
23. lo sgabello (loh sga-BEHL-loh)   stool
24. la mungitura (la moon-jee-TOO-ra)   milking
25. la zappa (la ZAP-pa)   hoe
26. il rastrello (eel ras-TREHL-loh)   rake
27. il forcone (eel fohr-KOH-nay)   pitchfork
28. la pala (la PA-la)   shovel
29. la pecora (la PEH-koh-ra)   sheep
30. il tacchino (eel tak-KEE-noh)   turkey
31. l'oca (LO-ka)   goose

32. **il prato irrigato** (eel PRA-toh eer-ree-GA-toh) irrigated field
33. **il spaventapasseri** (eel spa-vayn-ta-PAS-say-ree) scarecrow
34. **il trattore** (eel trat-TOH-ray) tractor
35. **il contadino** (eel kon-ta-DEE-noh) field hand
36. **il silo** (eel SEE-loh) silo
37. **il fienile** (eel fyeh-NEE-lay) loft
38. **il fango** (eel FAN-goh) mud
39. **il porco** (eel POR-koh) hog
40. **il porcile** (eel pohr-CHEE-lay) pigpen
41. **il pollaio** (eel pohl-LIGH-oh) chicken coop
42. **la gallina** (la gal-LEE-na) hen
43. **il cancello** (eel kan-CHEHL-loh) gate
44. **la carriola** (la kar-ree-O-la) wheelbarrow
45. **lo spruzzatore antiparassitario** (la sproo-tsa-TOH-ray an-tee-pa-ras-see-TA-ree-oh) fruit sprayer
46. **il sacco di grano** (eel SAK-koh dee GRA-noh) bag of wheat
47. **la capra** (la KAP-ra) goat
48. **l'erba** (LEHR-ba) grass
49. **il pozzo** (eel POT-tsoh) well
50. **la cascina** (la ka-SHEE-na) farmhouse

Questions

1. Who is milking the cow?
2. Where are horses kept?
3. Name all the animals on the farm.
4. What do you call the place where hogs are kept?

17. Gli animali allo zoo (lyee a-nee-MA-lee AL-oh zoo)
Animals in the Zoo

1. **la giraffa** (la jee-RAF-fa)   giraffe
2. **l'elefante** (leh-lay-FAN-tay)   elephant
3. **la zebra** (la ZEH-bra)   zebra
4. **la marmotta** (la mar-MOT-ta)   marmot
5. **il cervo** (eel CHER-voh)   deer
6. **il leone** (eel lee-OH-nay)   lion
7. **il gattopardo** (eel gat-toh-PAR-doh)   leopard

8. **il pappagallo** (eel pap-pa-GAL-loh)   parrot
9. **il quetzal** (eel kayt-ZAL)   quetzal
10. **il rinoceronte** (eel ree-noh-chay-ROHN-tay)   rhinoceros
11. **il koala** (eel koh-AL-a)   koala
12. **il serpente** (eel sehr-PEHN-tay)   snake
13. **lo scimpanzé** (loh sceem-pan-ZAY)   chimpanzee
14. **l'orso bianco** (LOHR-soh BYAN-ko)   polar bear

Questions

1. Name an animal with a very long neck.
2. Which animal lives in the Arctic?
3. Name two birds in the picture.
4. Which animal has antlers?

18. La spiaggia (la SPYA-ja)   The Beach

1. **i palazzi** (ee pa-LAT-tsee)   apartment buildings
2. **il faro** (eel FA-roh)   lighthouse
3. **l'isola** (LEE-zoh-la)   island
4. **il motoscafo** (eel moh-tohs-KA-foh)   speedboat
5. **il molo** (eel MO-loh)   pier
6. **il bagnino** (eel ba-NYEE-noh)   lifeguard
7. **il cocco** (eel KOHK-koh)   coconut
8. **il litorale** (eel lee-toh-RA-lay)   seashore
9. **il nuotatore** (eel nooh-ta-TOH-ray)   swimmer
10. **la tavoletta da surf** (la ta-voh-LAYT-ta da serf)   surfboard
11. **l'andare a cavallo** (lan-DA-ray a ka-VAL-loh)   horseback riding
12. **la macchina fotografica** (la MAK-kee-na foh-toh-GRA-fee-ka)   camera
13. **il legno trasportato dalla corrente**
    (eel LAY-nyoh tras-pohr-TA-toh DAL-la kohr-REHN-tay)   driftwood
14. **la radio portabile** (la RA-dyoh pohr-TA-bee-lay)   portable radio
15. **la sabbia** (la SAB-bya)   sand
16. **la sedia a sdraio** (la SEH-dya a SDRIGH-oh)   lounge chair
17. **l'ombrellone** (loh-brayl-LOH-nay)   beach umbrella
18. **il picnic** (eel PEEK-neek)   picnic
19. **il thermos** (eel TEHR-mohs)   thermos
20. **la crema abbronzante** (la CREH-ma ab-brohn-ZAN-tay)   suntan lotion
21. **il pallone** (eel pal-LOH-nay)   beach ball
22. **l'orma** (LOHR-ma)   footprint

23. **la conchiglia** (la kohn-KEE-lya)   sea shell
24. **l'alga marina** (LAL-ga ma-REE-na)   seaweed
25. **l'ostrica** (LO-stree-ka)   clam
26. **il castello di sabbia** (eel kas-TEHL-loh dee SAB-bya)   sand castle
27. **le pinne** (lay PEEN-nay)   fins
28. **il salvagente** (eel sal-va-JEN-tay)   lifesaver
29. **la maschera subacquea** (la MAS-kay-ra soob-ak-KWAY-a)   goggles
30. **la palma** (la PAL-ma)   palm tree
31. **l'asciugamano** (la-shoo-ga-MA-noh)   beach towel
32. **il remo** (eel REH-moh)   oar
33. **la barca a remo** (la BAR-ka a REH-moh)   rowboat
34. **il gabbiano** (eel GAB-bya-noh)   sea gull
35. **la foca** (la FO-ka)   seal
36. **il canotto pneumatico** (eel ka-NOT-toh pnayoo-MA-tee-koh)   inflatable boat
37. **l'otaria** (loh-TA-rya)   sea lion
38. **l'onda** (LOHN-da)   wave
39. **la capanna** (la ka-PAN-na)   hut
40. **la barca a vela** (la BAR-ka a VAY-la)   sailboat
41. **lo sci nautico** (loh shee NOW-tee-koh)   waterskiing
42. **la nave** (la NA-vay)   ocean liner

Questions

1. What do you call an umbrella that protects you from the sun?
2. What are the children building?
3. Name the animals on the beach.
4. Where is "il faro" located?

19. Il circo (eel CHEER-koh)   The Circus

1. **la verticale sulla testa** (la vayr-tee-KA-lay SOOL-la taysta)   headstand
2. **gli acrobati** (lyee ak-RO-ba-tee)   acrobats
3. **la tigre** (la TEE-gray)   tiger
4. **il fuoco** (eel FOOH-ko)   fire
5. **il cerchio di fuoco** (eel CHAYR-key-oh dee FOOH-koh)   ring of fire
6. **la frusta** (la FROOS-ta)   whip
7. **il domatore** (eel doh-ma-TOH-ray)   trainer
8. **il leone** (eel lay-OH-nay)   lion
9. **la corda di sicurezza** (la KOR-da dee see-koo-RAYT-tsa)   safety cord
10. **la cintura di sicurezza** (la cheen-TOO-ra dee see-koo-RAYT-tsa)   safety belt
11. **la cavallerizza senza sella** (la ka-val-lay-REET-tsa SAYN-za SEHL-la)
    bareback rider
12. **le piume** (lay PYOO-may)   feathers
13. **il costume** (eel kohs-TOO-may)   costume
14. **lo zucchero filato** (loh ZOOK-kay-roh fee-LA-toh)   cotton candy
15. **il pagliaccio** (eel pa-LYA-choh)   clown

16. **gli spettatori** (lyee spayt-ta-TOH-ree)   audience
17. **la parata** (la pa-RA-ta)   parade
18. **il monociclo** (eel mohn-noh-CHEEK-loh)   unicycle
19. **la corda tesa per funamboli** (la KOR-da TAY-sa payr foo-NAM-boh-lee)
    tightrope
20. **la rete di sicurezza** (la RAY-tay dee see-koo-RAYT-tsa)   safety net
21. **la scala di corda** (la SKA-la dee KOR-da)   rope ladder
22. **il presentatore** (eel pray-sayn-ta-TOH-ray)   master of ceremonies
23. **l'asta** (LAS-ta)   pole
24. **il trapezio** (eel tra-PEH-zyoh)   trapeze
25. **il trapezista** (eel tra-pay-ZEE-sta)   trapeze artist

Questions

1. Who is going through "il cerchio di fuoco"?
2. What is the boy in the audience eating?
3. What is the tightrope walker riding?
4. What object does the trainer have in his hand?

20. Gli strumenti musicali (lyee stroo-MAYN-tee moo-zee-KA-lee)
   Musical Instruments

1. **la chitarra** (la kee-TAR-ra)   guitar
2. **la maraca** (la ma-RA-ka)   maracas
3. **il timpano** (eel TEE-pa-noh)   kettledrum
4. **le nacchere** (lay NAK-kay-ray)   castanets
5. **la tromba** (la TROHM-ba)   trumpet
6. **il tamburello** (eel tam-boor-EHL-loh)   tambourine

7. **il violino** (eel vyoh-LEE-noh)   violin
8. **il contrabbasso** (eel kon-tra-BA-soh)   bass
9. **il mandolino** (eel man-doh-LEE-noh)   mandolin
10. **il basso** (eel BAS-soh)   baritone
11. **l'arpa** (LAR-pa)   harp
12. **il bangio** (eel BAN-joh)   banjo
13. **il sassofono** (eel sas-soh-FOH-noh)   saxophone
14. **il clarinetto** (eel kla-ree-NAYT-toh)   clarinet
15. **il pianoforte** (eel pya-noh-FOR-tay)   piano
16. **il trombone** (eel trohm-BOH-nay)   trombone

Questions

1. Name six instruments with strings.
2. Name five wind instruments.
3. What is "il timpano"?
4. Name an instrument that has a keyboard.

21. Le parole di movimento (le pa-ROH-lay dee moh-vee-MAYN-toh)
Action Words

1. **dondolare** (dohn-doh-LA-ray)   to swing
2. **scrivere** (SKREE-vay-ray)   to write
3. **ballare** (bal-LA-ray)   to dance
4. **mangiare** (man-JA-ray)   to eat
5. **sognare** (soh-NYA-ray)   to dream
6. **disegnare** (dee-say-NYA-ray)   to draw

7. **giocare** (joh-KA-ray)   to play
8. **lavorare** (la-voh-RA-ray)   to work
9. **pattinare** (pat-tee-NA-ray)   to skate
10. **andare in bicicletta** (an-DA-ray een bee-chee-KLAY-ta)   to ride a bicycle
11. **stirarsi** (stee-RAR-see)   to stretch

Questions

1. What do you do before playing a sport?
2. What do you do with a pencil?
3. What do you do with skates?
4. What is "ballare"?

22. I numeri (ee NOO-may-ree)   Numbers

1. **uno** (OO-noh)   one
2. **due** (DOO-ee)   two
3. **tre** (tray)   three
4. **quattro** (KWAT-troh)   four
5. **cinque** (CHEEN-kway)   five
6. **sei** (sehee)   six
7. **sette** (SEHT-tay)   seven
8. **otto** (OT-toh)   eight
9. **nove** (NO-vay)   nine
10. **dieci** (DYAY-chee)   ten

Questions

1. How many strawberries are there in the picture?
2. How many lemons are there in the picture?
3. How many flowers do you see in the picture?
4. How many peaches do you see?

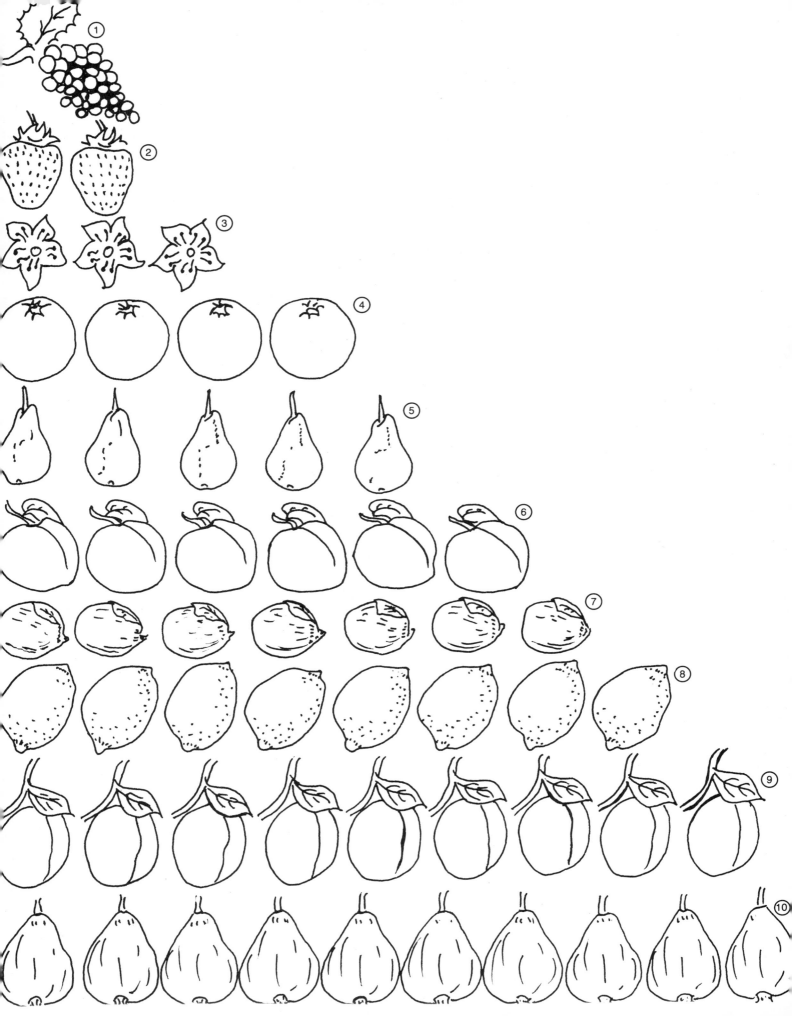

23. Le forme (lay FOHR-may) Shapes

1. **il quadrato** (eel kwa-DRA-toh) square
2. **il rombo** (eel ROHM-boh) rhombus
3. **la stella** (la STAYL-la) star
4. **l'ovale** (loh-VA-lay) oval
5. **il triangolo** (eel tree-AN-goh-loh) triangle
6. **il cerchio** (eel CHAYR-kee-oh) circle
7. **il rettangolo** (eel rayt-TAN-goh-loh) rectangle
8. **la mezzaluna** (la mayd-dza-LOO-na) crescent

Questions

1. Name three shapes that have four sides.
2. Name one shape that has three sides.
3. Which shape looks like a star?
4. What is "il cerchio"?

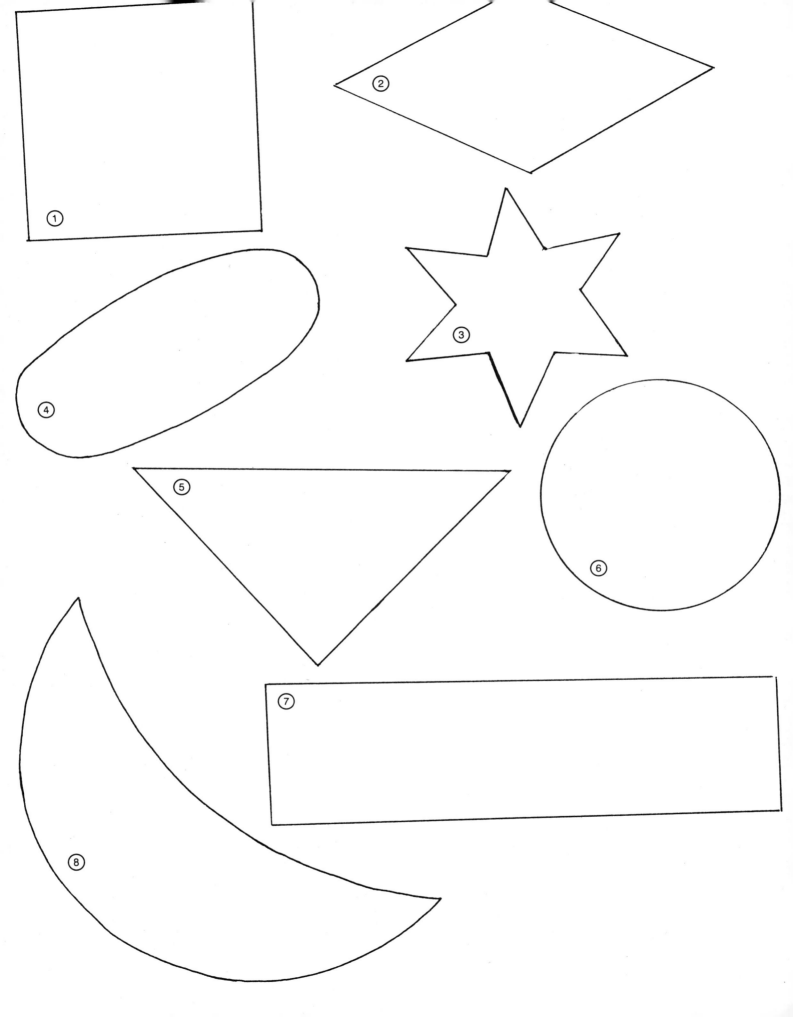

Risposte alle domande / Answers to the Questions

1. La nostra casa

1. il muro di mattoni, lo steccato
2. la paletta, il forchettone
3. per innaffiare piante, fiori (to water plants, flowers)
4. il giardiniere

2. Il salotto

1. il giornale, la lettera, la busta
2. i ferri da calza
3. il nipote
4. l'orologio
5. il libro

3. La cucina

1. il roastbeef
2. l'acqua
3. il toast
4. il cencio
5. il ricettario, il misurino, la scodella, il frullino a mano, i cucchiai per misurare, il setaccio

4. Nell'aula

1. le forbici
2. l'addizione, la sottrazione, la moltiplicazione
3. il grembiule
4. il dinosauro, l'orologio, la foto, il calendario, i disegni

5. I vestiti

1. gli occhiali
2. il pigiama
3. le calze
4. il costume da bagno

6. Le stagioni e il tempo

1. l'arcobaleno
2. l'estate
3. il fulmine
4. la luna

7. Gli sport

1. il baseball
2. lo sci, lo sci nautico
3. il ciclismo
4. il tennis, il bowling, la pallacanestro, il football americano, il baseball

8. La città

1. la collisione
2. l'ambulanza
3. il poliziotto
4. a fire fighter

9. Al supermercato

1. il gelato
2. le ciliege, le carote, le cipolle, i cavoli, i cavolfiori
3. la cassiera
4. il carrello
5. il sacco di carta

10. Al ristorante

1. il cuoco
2. la cameriera
3. il panino
4. il menu
5. il tovagliolo

11. La posta

1. la posta
2. il francobollo
3. il postino
4. a newspaper

12. La banca

1. la carta di credito, l'assegno
2. la cassaforte
3. il custode
4. il modulo per i depositi

13. Dal medico

1. l'infermiere
2. lo stetoscopio
3. il veterinario
4. crutches
5. la ricetta

14. La stazione di servizio

1. il meccanico
2. bumper
3. il carro attrezzi
4. l'autolavaggio
5. il bagagliaio

15. Il trasporto

1. il paracadute
2. la motocicletta, la bicicletta
3. il sottomarino
4. il missile

16. La fattoria

1. la contadina
2. la stalla
3. il toro, il cavallo, la mucca,
   la pecora, il tacchino, l'oca, il porco,
   la gallina, la capra
4. il porcile

17. Gli animali allo zoo

1. la giraffa
2. l'orso bianco
3. il pappagallo, il quetzal
4. il cervo

18. La spiaggia

1. l'ombrellone
2. il castello di sabbia
3. il cavallo, l'ostrica, il gabbiano,
   la foca
4. sull'isola

19. Il circo

1. la tigre
2. lo zucchero filato
3. il monociclo
4. la frusta

20. Gli strumenti musicali

1. la chitarra, il violino, il contrabbasso,
   il mandolino, l'arpa, il bangio
2. la tromba, il basso, il sassofono,
   il clarinetto, il trombone
3. kettledrum
4. il pianoforte

21. Le parole di movimento

1. stirarsi
2. scrivere
3. pattinare
4. dance

22. I numeri

1. due
2. otto
3. tre
4. sei

23. Le forme

1. il quadrato, il rombo, il rettangolo
2. il triangolo
3. la stella
4. circle